DROUGHT IN THE PARADISE

MOOMIN BASHIR

Contents

Contents

Contents

Contents

1. The Symphony of Tomorrow

I love the way you breathe,
A whisper in the night,
Soft and steady, bringing peace,
A rhythm pure and light.
I love the way you think,
Thoughts that dance and weave,
A mind that's full of wonders,
Inspiration you conceive.
I love the way you walk,
Each step a graceful art,
With confidence and purpose,
That captivates my heart,
I love the way you talk,
Your voice a soothing stream,
Each word a melody,
A comfort and a dream.
I love the way you eat,
Savoring each bite,
With joy and appreciation,
Turning meals to pure delight
I love the way you smile,
A beacon in the gloom,

A light that fills my world,
And makes the flowers bloom.
I love the way you drink,
So elegant and true,
Each sip a silent symphony,
A part of you, anew.
In every move and moment,
A beauty deep and true,
A symphony of simple things,
That makes me cherish you.

2. Silent Devotion

In quiet shadows, where dreams entwine,
My heart reveals a truth so fine.
Though words between us seldom flow,
My love for you still softly glows.
I may not send you texts each day,
Yet in my mind, you always stay.
Your messages, like whispers sweet,
I answer with my heart's own beat.
I may not greet you with the dawn,
But you're the first I think upon.
And as the night enfolds its shroud,
Your face appears among the clouds.
Each morning's light, each evening's sigh,
Carries your name to the sky.
My love, unspoken, deep and true,
Forever finds its way to you.
For though we walk on separate ways,
My heart's a compass, still it sways,
To where you are, both night and day,
In dreams and thoughts, you always stay.
I cannot move, nor wish to flee,
This love that binds so tenderly.
Though silent be my lips to thee,

My soul proclaims, eternally.

3. Forever Yours

Under the stars, where dreams ignite,
In the glow of love's soft light,
With every beat, my heart will say,
Will you be mine, come what may?
Like petals dance upon the breeze,
Your love has brought me to my knees,
With this ring, I pledge to you,
A love that's pure, a love that's true.
So here and now, with all my soul,
I ask you, love, to make me whole,
Will you share with me life's journey,
And be forever my one and only?"

4. Echoes of Forgotten Land….!

The land now weeps, its beauty frayed.

Walls of concrete, hearts encased,

A dream of peace, so swiftly erased.

In Palestine, the sun sets red,

Upon a land where so much has bled.

Homes demolished, lives torn asunder,

Under skies filled with endless thunder.

A mother cries, her tears like rain,

For a son who won't come home again.

The world looks on, a silent bystander,

To the cries from Gaza, growing grander

In Kashmir, the valleys whisper low,

Of tales of sorrow, pain, and woe.

Mountains tall, their silence breached,

By the cries of those, freedom beseeched.

A land divided, hearts entwined,

In a dance of sorrow, hopes confined.

The rivers flow with silent screams,

Of lives disrupted, shattered dreams.

A father holds a picture tight,

Of a daughter lost in the dead of night.

The world looks on, indifferent gaze,

To the cries of Kashmir, in a foggy haze.
Two lands, two tales of grief profound,
Echoes of history, so tightly wound.
Injustice reigns where love should grow,
In Palestine and Kashmir, the pain does flow.
The world debates, its conscience dulled,
While in these lands, hope is culled.
Yet still they rise, with voices strong,
In the face of wrong, they carry on.
For in the hearts of those oppressed,
Lives a flame that can't be repressed.
Palestine, Kashmir, your cries we hear,
In solidarity, we stand near.

5. Cynicisms VEIL

Beneath a sky so vast and grey,

Where sunlight's truth has gone astray,

A shadow lurks in every heart,

A whispered doubt, a skeptic's art.

Once, dreams were woven, bright and bold,

In innocence, tales of gold,

But time has sharpened every edge,

And left us teetering on a ledge.

Eyes now see with jaded hue,

Trust but a relic, tried and true,

Every smile a mask, a feigned delight,

In the theater of an endless night.

Promises break like fragile glass,

Words like winds through canyons pass,

We build our walls, stone by stone,

In a world where we walk alone.

Hope, a distant, fleeting star,

Faith, a bruise, a lasting scar,

We learn to shield, to doubt, to hide,

In cynicism, our trusted guide.

Yet in this realm of shadowed thought,

A seed of truth can still be sought,

For in the darkness, light can grow,

A spark of faith, a gentle glow.
Perhaps in doubting, we can find,
A deeper truth, a wiser mind,
To see the world, not black and white,
But shades of gray in soft twilight.
And though cynicism clouds our view,
In its shadows, courage too,
To question, seek, and redefine,
The boundaries of this heart of mine.

6. Struggle of Father

In quiet strength, you stood so tall,
A guiding light through life's long hall.
With gentle words and steady hands,
You taught me how to understand.
Your wisdom shared in simple ways,
A beacon through my darkest days.
In laughter, tears, and dreams we chase,
You've shaped my life with boundless grace.
Though time may pass and seasons change,
The bond we share will still remain.
A father's love, so pure and true,
Forever lives in all I do.

2.

Abu

In the quiet hours before dawn,
I remember your hands,
Rough from years of labor,
Cradling my dreams like fragile birds.
You wore your struggle like a second skin,
Each wrinkle a testament to battles fought,
Each callus a badge of honor.
The world weighed heavy on your shoulders,
Yet you carried it, with a strength that seemed unbreakable.

Your love was not in words,

But in actions,

In the way you rose before the sun,

The way you toiled in fields and factories,

The way you sacrificed silently,

So I could soar free.

Now, in the echoing halls of my hostel,

I feel the void where your presence used to be,

A chasm that swallows the comfort of home.

The walls whisper your absence,

Each creak and groan a reminder,

Of the distance between us.

I miss the smell of your cooking,

The stories you told in your quiet voice,

The laughter that bubbled up from deep within you,

Even on the hardest days.

I miss the way you looked at me,

With pride that lit up your tired eyes.

.Here, surrounded by strangers,

I carry pieces of you with me,

A patchwork quilt of memories,

Stitched together with love and longing.

Your lessons echo in my mind,

Your strength fuels my resolve,

And though I am far,

Your spirit walks beside me.

Abu, your struggle was your gift,

A legacy of resilience and love.

In the silence of my solitude,

I hear your voice,

A steady heartbeat,

Guiding me through the darkness.

7. Responsibilities

In the labyrinth of teen life's maze,
Where every turn brings new ways,
Echoes of dreams and hopes arise,
Beneath the vast and changing skies.
Bound by threads of family's grace,
Guiding steps in life's swift race,
Expectations whisper, steadfast and strong,
Urging paths where dreams belong.
Between the lines of youthful years,
Echoes of laughter, joy, and tears,
Navigating choices, wise and bold,
As stories of the past are retold.
In the clash of old and new,
In every path we dare pursue,
The dance of expectation and desire,
Fuels the teenage heart with fire.
Yet in the balance, we strive to find,
A place where hearts and souls align,
Where dreams take flight on winds of grace,
In the journey of life's destined race.

8. Mother

In the quiet dawn, she rises,

Her steps gentle as whispers on a breeze,

Each motion a dance of devotion,

A symphony of selfless love.

Her hands, weathered yet tender,

Cradle the world with care,

Guiding, nurturing, crafting dreams

In the soft light of morning prayers

Her eyes, windows to a soul vast and kind,

Gaze upon us with unwavering faith,

Seeing not just who we are,

But who we might become.

Through the storms and sunshine,

Her voice remains a beacon,

A lullaby in the darkest night,

A call to courage in the light of day.

Her heart, a boundless ocean,

Holds the secrets of countless sacrifices,

Stories etched in the silence

Of nights spent in quiet toil.

In every act of kindness, In every word of wisdom,

She plants the seeds of Paradise,

For it is said, and truly believed,

That Paradise lives underneath your feet,

Mother, A haven of eternal peace.

In the soft shadows of your presence,

We find our way, Grateful for each step you take,

Leading us gently, ever toward the light.

9. Alvida

My heart once held your cherished name,
In dreams that sparkled, flickered, flame.
Reflections now of days gone by,
Moments lost like whispers, sigh.
All you sought were selfish ends,
Ruptured trust that time won't mend.
I wish you well, as paths diverge,
A life to live, without this surge.
Magnolias bloomed in gardens vast,
In the echoes of our past.
Radiant, your smile did gleam,
Mirroring a fleeting dream.
Amidst the shadows, truths unveil,
Revelations in the veil.
I beheld a love so pure,
A beacon bright, yet insecure.
Nebulous are ties that bind,
Obscured now in the corridors of mind.
Oblivion calls, yet I resist,
Resolute, though feelings twist.
Recollections weave a tapestry,
Stitched with threads of you and me.
Time, relentless, marches on,

Leaving remnants, dusk to dawn.

Ambivalence now fills the void,

Memories both cherished and destroyed.

I wish you well, though hearts do ache,

As we each our paths must take.

Radiance follows in your wake,

Illuminate the steps you take.

Adieu, my love, as I depart,

Nevermore to share a heart.

In twilight's gentle, soft embrace,

Out of sight, but not erased.

Oaths once spoken, now no more,

Rendered silent, on distant shores.

Requiem for a love once bright,

Stay safe, live true, within the light.

10. How jealous the moon was

How jealous the moon became of my love,
How it whispered through the night from above.
"How dare you let her walk under my light,
When she outshines the stars in her own right."
The moon, with its silvery, envious glow,
Watched her beauty in the soft twilight's flow.
"She rivals my splendor, it just isn't fair,
That such a wonder walks under my stare."
Her eyes, like stars, sparkle brighter than mine,
In her presence, the night can only pine.
"How dare she steal my silent night's grace,
With every soft whisper, with each tender trace."
The moon's soft beams, they tried to compete,
But her radiance made their efforts incomplete.
"Oh, jealous am I, hung high in the sky,
That such a beauty should cause me to sigh."
Yet, as I held her close under the night's dome,
I knew that with her, my heart found its home.
"Let the moon be jealous," I whispered with glee,
"For no light compares to the love she gives me."

11. Her

In the quiet of the twilight's glow,
Her beauty blossoms, subtle and low.
A smile that lights the evening's shade,
With secrets in her eyes, softly laid.
Her laughter, a melody, gentle and clear,
Echoes through the night, drawing near.
Each word she speaks, a tender refrain,
Like whispers of love in a gentle rain.
Her presence, a painting, soft and bright,
A masterpiece hidden in plain sight.
In the gardens of her dreams, she roams,
A world of wonder, a place called home.
No one knows the secrets she keeps,
In the shadows where her heart leaps.
But I see the beauty, deep and true,
In every moment, in all she'll do.
For she is a mystery, lovely and rare,
With a heart so gentle, beyond compare.
In the quiet of the twilight's glow,
Her beauty blossoms, and I know.

12. Teens and responsibilities

In the twists and turns of teen life's maze,
Where every corner brings new days,
With dreams and hopes that never die,
Underneath the ever-changing sky.
Bound by the love of family's embrace,
Guiding steps in life's fast pace,
Expectations whisper, firm and clear,
Pushing us forward year by year.
Between the moments of laughter and tears,
Navigating choices, facing our fears,
Finding our way, trying to be bold,
As stories of our lives unfold.
In the clash of old ways and new,
In every path we choose to pursue,
The mix of hopes and expectations,
Fuels our hearts with determination.
Yet in the balance, we aim to find,
A place where hearts and minds are aligned,
Where dreams take flight, hopes interlace,
In the journey of life's destined race.

13. Lament of Hope

Once a beacon bright in endless night,
Guiding steps with tender light,
Hope, a fragile, fleeting flame,
Now whispers only shadows' name.
In fields where dreams once took their flight,
Now barren, empty, lost to sight,
A heart once filled with vibrant dreams,
Now echoes hollow, silent screams.
The dawn that promised new delight,
Now shrouds the world in endless plight,
Each day, a struggle, weary, worn,
A soul left tattered, faith forlorn.
Once the stars sang hymns of grace,
Now their silence fills the space,
Where once was laughter, joy, and song,
Now sorrow's dirge plays ever long.
The flame that once defied the dark,
Extinguished now, a lifeless spark,
In twilight's grasp, we mourn the fall,
Of hope that once stood proud and tall.
Yet in this darkness, deep and cold,
A whisper faint, a story told,
That even in the blackest night,

A glimmer waits to reignite.

For though hope wanes and fades from sight,

It lingers still, a stubborn light,

And though today we walk alone,

Tomorrow's dawn may yet atone.

14. Echoes of Everlasting LOVE

I want to talk to you, to hear your voice,

To feel you near, my heart's sole choice.

In silent nights, I long to see

Your smile, your words, comforting me.

I want you here, your presence warm,

To shield me from life's raging storm.

To listen close to all my sorrows,

And hug me tight, till better tomorrows.

You'd call me "duffer" with a gentle laugh,

A promise that you'd always have

My back, my heart, in darkest days,

Your love, your light, in countless ways.

But now you're gone, so far away,

In memories, your essence stays.

I miss you more with every breath,

A void within, a heart bereft.

Yet in the silence, I hear your cheer,

A whisper soft: "I'm always near."

15. Echoes of good bye

In the shadows of silence, I dwell,
As memories of her departure swell.
A void within, where once she'd reside,
Now echoes the emptiness of the tide.
Whispers of her laughter, now a distant song,
In the corridors of my heart, they long.
With every passing breeze, I feel her absence keen,
A kaleidoscope of emotions, unseen.
Her absence paints the sky with hues of gray,
As I navigate through the ruins of yesterday.
Yet, in the ruins, a flicker of hope does gleam,
That someday, from this pain, I'll redeem.
Though she left, her essence lingers still,
In the quiet moments, I feel her gentle thrill.
But in the tapestry of life, new threads shall weave,
As I learn to heal and to believe.
So, here I stand, amidst the echoes of goodbye,
Finding solace in the tears I cry.
For in the wake of her departure, I find,
The strength to embrace what's left behind.

16. In The Echoes Of HER Text

Once, she texted me, and I replied,
And from there, we ascended to paradise.
Each day she wove beauty and grace,
Unforgettable memories in every embrace.
She made each moment a cherished gift,
Days filled with joy, my spirits lift.
With her, life sparkled, a radiant hue,
She gave me purpose, and motivation too.
But then, like a sudden, stormy gale,
She left, and it felt like I fell without a sail.
From the heights of happiness, I plunged deep,
As if I fell from the Burj Khalifa's peak.
Her absence echoes in each quiet room,
A void so vast, like eternal gloom.
Yet, I'll hold onto the memories we shared,
In the echoes of her text, I find she still cared.
Though she's gone, her light remains,
In my heart, where love forever sustains.
I'll cherish the beauty she brought to me,
In the echoes of her text, I'll always be.
So, as I stand in the shadow of loss,
I remember the paradise, the joy, the gloss.

For she brought me to life, set me free,
In the echoes of her text, she'll forever be.

17. Battles in the Shadow

At sixteen, he leaves the nest,
A dream in his eyes, a fire in his chest,
To conquer exams, to reach for the stars,
He ventures alone, leaving familiar bars.
In a hostel's cold, unfeeling embrace,
He fights silent battles, finds his own place.
No friends to lean on, no family near,
He cloaks his fears, swallows each tear.
Some days are lean, no money in hand,
Nights spent hungry, with dreams he can't stand.
But to parents back home, he speaks not a word,
For their peace of mind, his pain stays unheard.
In the quiet of night, in his solitary room,
He weeps unseen, in the echoing gloom.
"I'm not enough," his heart silently screams,
As he battles self-doubt, tears apart dreams.
But despite the pain, he rises each day,
With a spirit unbroken, finding his way.
For in the heart of his struggle, a warrior's birth,
Forging his path, defining his worth.
The road is hard, the journey long,
Yet in his silence, he grows strong.
One day, he'll emerge, from battles won,

A testament to the strength of a solitary son.

18. The day of Reckoning

In the dawn of timeless grace, the sky shall rend,
And light shall flood the Earth, where shadows blend.
The trumpet's call, so loud and clear, will sound,
Reviving souls, from graves unbound.
Each heart laid bare, each deed exposed to light,
No secret kept, no sin concealed from sight.
The scales of justice balanced in His hand,
Deciding fates with wisdom, pure and grand.
The righteous rise, their faces shining bright,
With hearts as pure as morning's first light.
Their deeds, a bridge to paradise they stride,
Where rivers flow, and endless joys abide.
But those whose hearts were veiled in darkest night,
Who turned from truth, who shunned the guiding light,
Shall face the fire, where shadows never cease,
Their cries for mercy swallowed by the beast.
The day of reckoning, where destinies entwine,
Where mercy meets with justice, the divine.
In this great hour, we stand to face our fate,
The paradise of peace, or hell's dark gate.
So live with kindness, let your heart be true,
For on that day, it's deeds that will renew.
In every moment, choose the righteous way,

Prepare for resurrection's fateful day.

19. Beyond the Horizon

When mountains rise and paths are steep,
And shadows gather where dreams sleep,
Take heart, young soul, and forge ahead,
With courage strong and fears unfed.
For every challenge, every test,
Is but a step toward your best.
The doubts may whisper, loud and clear,
But let your spirit persevere.
Push past the limits, break the chains,
Embrace the sun, outshine the rains.
For in your heart, a fire glows,
A strength untapped, a force that grows.
Remember those who watch and pray,
Who cheer you on, night and day.
Your parents' hopes, their silent pride,
In every tear, in every stride.
Through sleepless nights and endless days,
Through winding roads and uncharted ways,
You carve your path, you find your light,
And turn the darkness into bright.
So rise, young warrior, face the fight,
With dreams as vast as the starry night.
For every step, a victory won,

In every heart, the proud beats run.

And when the summit stands in view,

With skies of endless, boundless blue,

Know that your journey, brave and true,

Has made your parents proud of you.

20. After SHE left

The door closed softly, echoes in the night,
A silence followed, stealing all the light.
Her presence gone, a shadow in her place,
A hollow ache, a vacant space.
My heart, once full, now heavy with the void,
A symphony of sorrow, love destroyed.
The laughter, memories, now seem so far,
Like distant whispers, faint and marred.
I wander through the days, a ghostly guise,
With empty arms and tear-streaked eyes.
The world moves on, but I stand still,
A hollow shell, against my will.
Her touch, her voice, a lingering ghost,
In quiet moments, I miss the most.
Each corner holds a piece of her,
A haunting presence, a silent blur.
Yet through this hollow, I will find,
The strength to heal, the peace of mind.
For though she's gone, her love remains,
A bittersweet, enduring pain.
In time, the void may start to fill,
With new beginnings, against my will.
But for now, I mourn, I grieve, I yearn,

For her return, a love to burn.
The hollow lingers, deep and wide,
But with each step, I find my stride.
For even hollow, I still stand,
With hope and heart, I mend the strands.

21. She made me realize my worth

In her eyes, I saw a light so bright,

A reflection of my soul, a beacon in the night.

She showed me the value of my heart and mind,

And made me realize my worth, so divine.

Her touch ignited a fire within,

A flame that burned away my doubts and sin.

She showed me that I was worthy of love,

And that my dreams and aspirations were from above.

With her by my side, I felt complete,

A sense of purpose, a sense of beat.

She helped me see the beauty in myself,

And made me realize my worth, my wealth.

In her arms, I found my home,

A place where I could be myself, and be unknown.

She showed me that I was enough,

And that my worth was not based on luck.

So here I'll stay, in her loving embrace,

Where I've found my worth, my place, my grace.

For she has made me realize my worth,

And I am forever grateful, forever death.

22. When she was within me

She walked into my life, like a sunny day
Bringing joy and laughter, in every way
Her smile could light up the night
And make my heart sing with delight
She made my life a memory, so sweet and true
With every moment, my love for her grew
In her eyes, I saw a shining light
That made my heart take flight
She was my everything, my guiding star
The one who made my life so far
From the moment I met her, I knew
That my heart would forever be true
She made my life a memory, so precious and rare
With her by my side, I knew I'd always be there
Together we'd dance, under the stars above
And our love would forever be a labor of love

23. Shadows of Silence

In lands where ancient whispers dwell,
Where stories of old and tears compel,
There lies a shadow, dark and grim,
Of suffering that silences hymn.
Palestine's cry, a haunting plea,
Beneath olive trees, they yearn to be free.
Walls and bullets, tearing apart,
Homes and hearts, a fractured art.
Kashmir's valleys, draped in mist,
Echo with voices that cease to exist.
Mountains stand, as silent guards,
To a tale of sorrows, breaking hearts.
Innocent lives, dreams betrayed,
Under skies where freedom's delayed.
Mothers weep, their children gone,
In the twilight, their silent song.
Prayers linger in the night,
Hoping dawn will bring some light.
Yet the world turns a deaf ear,
To the cries that are so near.
Genocide's grip, a ruthless hand,
Strangles hope in every land.
Yet the spirit fights to rise,

Against the darkness, against the lies.
In Palestine and Kashmir's strife,
Flows the river of endless life.
Through tears and blood, they persevere,
With a courage that won't disappear.
So we remember, and we must speak,
For those whose voices have grown weak.
In solidarity, we must stand,
For peace and justice across the land.

24. Shadows of Silence

In the quiet corners of my mind,
Dreams of science, unconfined.
Equations dance, theories soar,
But family demands something more.
A boy they say, must bear the weight,
Of expectations, set by fate.
Engineering dreams, crushed beneath,
The pressure to pursue, to breathe.
"Biology," they insist, "is your path,"
Ignoring my passion, fueling my wrath.
A doctor's coat, they envision clear,
But my heart yearns for math, it's near.
Family's voice, a constant call,
Boys must rise, they must not fall.
Rigid paths and stern commands,
A future planned by their hands.
Through microscopes and cells I tread,
With a heavy heart, dreams almost dead.
But within me, a spark remains,
A silent protest against these chains.
In the night, I whisper low,
To the stars that seem to know,
The struggles of a heart confined,

By love that's harsh, yet intertwined.
One day, I'll break this mold,
Forge my path, be bold.
For now, I walk a line so thin,
Between duty's call and dreams within.
To every boy who feels this strain,
Know that dreams aren't in vain.
Fight for what sets your soul ablaze,
Through the fog, find your ways.
In silent battles, strength is found,
To rise above, to stand your ground.
For dreams deferred are not denied,
In your heart, let passions reside.

25. Masked smiles

In a world where boys must stand,
Strong and silent, by demand.
Behind the mask, a hidden tear,
A heart that battles constant fear.
Family's words, a heavy load,
On paths where dreams are coldly stowed.
"Be a man," they often say,
"Hide your pain, keep tears at bay.
"Pressure mounts, expectations high,
Yet through it all, they wear a smile.
A façade of strength, a cheerful guise,
While inside, a fragile heart lies.
Heartbreaks endured, silent screams,
Crushed beneath the weight of dreams.
Respect sought, yet hard to gain,
In a world that seldom sees their pain.
Family's talks, like daggers thrown,
Criticisms in a harsh tone.
Yet they nod, and bear the brunt,
Of every harsh and bitter front.
Boys who carry this silent ache,
In shadows, their resolve won't break.
With every smile, a story untold,

Of courage hidden, quietly bold.
They laugh and joke, play their part,
Concealing the wounds within their heart.
For the world demands a steadfast face,
While their spirit runs a secret race.
In their eyes, a flicker of fight,
A dream to chase, a guiding light.
Though weary from the battles fought,
Hope remains, a cherished thought.
To every boy who wears this mask,
Your strength is more than just a task.
Beneath the pressure, find your voice,
For in your truth, you'll find your choice.
One day the weight will lift away,
And you'll be free to seize the day.
Until then, know you're not alone,
In this silent struggle, you're known.

26. All eyes on RAFAH

In the land where olive trees once thrived,
Where children's laughter filled the skies,
Now echoes of sorrow and cries,
All eyes on Rafah, where innocence dies.
A city besieged by endless strife,
Where shadows dance with loss of life,
Tiny hands reach out in vain,
For dreams now buried under the pain.
The night descends with a fearful roar,
As bombs and bullets shatter the floor,
Homes turned to rubble, hearts to dust,
Trust eroded, lives unjust.
In Rafah's streets, the ghosts now roam,
Searching for peace, a distant home,
Yet amidst the tears and endless night,
A flicker of hope, a yearning for light.
We bear witness, we cannot turn away,
Their stories echo, their voices say:
Remember Rafah, remember the cost,
For in our silence, humanity's lost.

27. Lost Humanity in Robotic Age

In circuits' hum and algorithms' rise,
We chase the dawn of our machine-made dreams,
Yet in this quest, a part of us now dies,
Our values lost in cold, robotic schemes.
Advancement's light obscures the human touch,
In steel and code, compassion fades away,
We trade our hearts for wires and gears, as such,
The soul of man in silicon does sway.
What price we pay for progress' gleaming tide,
When empathy and kindness lay in waste,
A future where our moral compass hides,
And ethics, once so cherished, left displaced.
Amidst the whirr of progress, we forget,
The warmth of human bonds that once held true,
In this new age, a digital vignette,
Our sacred virtues seem to fade from view.
We build and build, yet lose the art to feel,
In endless code, our spirits drift away,
Forgetting what it means to truly heal,
Our hearts grow cold in artificial sway.
Oh, let us pause and seek what we have lost,
Lest humankind's true essence pay the cost.

28. Madness of JEE and NEET

In hallowed halls of endless preparation,
Young minds are trapped in cycles of despair,
Their dreams confined by tests and expectation,
A burden far too heavy now to bear.
The books, the tests, the nights that never end,
Where intellect is gauged by marks alone,
In classrooms where the light begins to bend,
And spirits wither, hearts turn into stone.
They feel the weight of futures on their backs,
Believing this is all they're meant to be,
In corridors where joy and hope now lack,
A single path, no room for liberty.
Parents press with love that turns to chain,
To crack the code, to reach the highest tier,
Not seeing how they feed into the pain,
Their children's worth reduced to scores and fear.
And judges, with their eyes on rank and grade,
Forget the souls behind the test results,
A world where worth is in percentages made,
And failure brands them lesser by default.
Oh, let us see beyond this mad façade,
Where true potential's lost in numbers' sway,

Embrace the light in every child's heart,
And guide them towards their own unique array.

29. Symphony of tomorrow

In realms where circuits breathe and pulse,
AI awakens, a silent waltz.
With code as its sinew, thought as its soul,
It learns, evolves, begins to console.
From the dawn of simple tasks at hand,
To complex realms, it starts to understand.
In kitchens, classrooms, cities bright,
AI's touch turns dark to light.
Humans and machines, a dance entwined,
In daily rhythms, futures aligned.
Guiding hands in tasks so small,
Solving puzzles, answering calls.
Advancements burst like stars unseen,
Breakthroughs bright in fields serene.
From health to art, from space to earth,
AI's spark ignites new birth.
Yet shadows cast in brightened day,
Ethical doubts in minds do weigh.
Privacy, security, autonomy's plight,
Questions that stir in the deep of night.
Employment's shift, a market turned,
Skills outdated, lessons learned.

Society bends, adapts with grace,
In AI's wake, new roles embrace.
Balance found in gifts it brings,
Challenges vast as future sings.
From curing ills to global peace,
AI's potential may never cease.
Yet forward gazing, futures wide,
Utopias dream, dystopias chide.
Humanity's hand must guide this fate,
To ensure all share in the promised state.
In wonder, caution, we reflect,
On what it means to be, to connect.
As AI grows, our hearts must see,
The blend of tech and humanity.
A symphony of man and machine,
A future bright, yet unforeseen.
Together we'll script tomorrow's lore,
In harmony forevermore.
In the age of circuits, wires, and code,
Where algorithms decipher the road,
We chase the stars, we touch the sky,
Yet often fail to question why.
Machines that think, and speak, and feel,
With metal hearts, and minds of steel,
They serve us well, they do our will,
But leave a void, a deeper chill.
In cities built on digital streams,

We lose ourselves in virtual dreams.
Neighbors become faces on a screen,
In a world where empathy grows lean.
We marvel at the AI's might,
Its power to transform the night,
But in its glow, a shadow grows,
The warmth of human touch, it knows.
Our duties fade in neon lights,
We turn away from simple rights.
The call of kindness, once so near,
Is drowned by progress, loud and clear.
Yet in this era, bright and grand,
We must remember to extend a hand,
To see the person, not the part,
To feel with soul, to love with heart.
For science, AI, and robots fine,
Are tools to serve, not to define.
Our essence lies in human grace,
In shared respect, in warm embrace.
So let us merge our quests for more,
With values that we can't ignore.
In every code, in every line,
Let's weave the threads of the divine.

30. The Silent Boy

In a world where shadows loom,
A boy walks in a quiet room.
Voices murmur, fingers point,
Yet he stands, with joints disjoint.
They say he's rough, they say he's cold,
A story spun, a tale retold.
No value seen in his pure heart,
His worth dismissed right from the start.
"Characterless," they cruelly claim,
A cheater, lust-driven, with no shame.
Behind desires, they say he hides,
In a sea of lies, his truth subsides.
The world insists he's always wrong,
His spirit trapped in silence long.
Judged for actions, words unspoken,
A broken soul, yet not broken.
They harass, they tease, they pry,
Under scrutiny's relentless eye.
Yet he resists, with silent might,
A boy in darkness, seeking light.
His character, a precious gem,
Ignored by those who can't see him.
Society talks, society shames,

Yet in his heart, a fire flames.

He bears the weight, he endures the pain,

A storm inside, a silent rain.

No uttered word, no voice to shout,

His strength within, a silent bout.

Through the whispers, through the scorn,

A boy remains, though weather-worn.

For in his silence, there's a roar,

A testament to something more.

In the end, when all is done,

A boy will rise like morning sun.

His silent strength, his quiet grace,

Will find its way, will find its place.

31. The Silent Struggle

In shadows cast by whispers cold,
A boy stands firm, his story untold.
A heart weighed down by unseen chains,
In a world that only sees his pains.
Fingers point, voices blame,
Calling him the source of shame.
Misunderstood, yet strong he stays,
Through the darkest, longest days.
Parents' hopes, a heavy load,
Dreams of success, a narrow road.
His path defined by others' eyes,
As silent tears fill his skies.
They say he's wrong, they say he's flawed,
Judged by rules that seem so broad.
His needs ignored, his cries unheard,
In silence, he swallows every word.
Yet in his heart, a fire burns,
A spirit strong, a soul that yearns.
For understanding, for a chance,
To live his life, to take his stance.
Let us see beyond the veil,
A boy's true worth, a different tale.
With kindness, let's break the mold,

And let his story, his truth be told.

In Shadows Cast by Whispers Cold

A boy stands firm, his story untold.

A heart weighed down by unseen chains,

In a world that only sees his pains.

Fingers Point, Voices Blame

Calling him the source of shame.

Misunderstood, yet strong he stays,

Through the darkest, longest days.

Parents' Hopes, a Heavy Load

Dreams of success, a narrow road.

His path defined by others' eyes,

As silent tears fill his skies.

They Say He's Wrong, They Say He's Flawed

Judged by rules that seem so broad.

Called characterless, full of lust,

Their harsh words turn dreams to dust.

His Needs Ignored, His Cries Unheard

In silence, he swallows every word.

Yet in his heart, a fire burns,

A spirit strong, a soul that yearns.

For Understanding, for a Chance

To live his life, to take his stance.

Let us see beyond the veil,

A boy's true worth, a different tale.

With Kindness, Let's Break the Mold

And let his story, his truth be told.

32. Stereotype about boys

In a world of rigid lines and creeds,
Boys are cast in roles decreed.
Strong and stoic, brave and bold,
In a mold that's centuries old.
"Big boys don't cry," they say,
"Man up, stand tall, don't sway."
But hearts inside are tender, too,
Boys feel pain, and joys, and blues.
Society's gaze is hard and stern,
Boys mustn't falter, they must learn,
To hide their tears, to veil their fears,
To bury doubts through the years.
But boys are more than rugged might,
They dream, they wonder, they take flight.
They love deeply, they care, they feel,
Their hearts are open, wounds are real.
So let us break these chains so tight,
Allow boys to be in their own right.
To show emotions, to be free,
To live in truth and authenticity.
For in their souls, diverse and vast,
Lies the future, unbound by the past.
Boys, unconfined by stereotype's glance,

Deserve the world, a fairer chance.

33. The path of TRIUMPH

In the quiet hours of dawn's first light,

The pages turn, a journey to begin.

Each line and word, a challenge to ignite,

A fire within, determination's kin.

The path is steep, with trials that test the soul,

Yet through the night, your spirit must not fade.

In every heartbeat, find your destined goal,

With each small victory, let progress be made.

The doubts may creep, like shadows in the mind,

But courage stands, a beacon in the dark.

With focused will, leave hesitation behind,

Embrace the grind, ignite your inner spark.

For in this quest, your dreams shall find their place,

Through sweat and toil, you'll earn your rightful space.

34. Reflections of the jhelum

By the Jhelum's bank in Rajbagh fair,
I watched the people with vacant stare.
Fake smiles they wore, a daily guise,
Hiding the hunger in their eyes.
Some hurried back to nests unseen,
Their silent struggles, the Jhelum's sheen.
Others feasted, yet starved inside,
No joy in their hearts, no peace to bide.
Amongst the crowd, an odd one found,
Students with anxiety all around.
A-graders, C-graders, no difference shown,
Each in their worries, silently alone.
Some found solace in friendship's grace,
Others in a lover's embrace.
Yet all were burdened by unseen chains,
The river flowed, absorbing their pains.
By Jhelum's bank, life's fragile art,
Each smile a mask, hiding the heart.
In Rajbagh's calm, the truth lay bare,
A world of faces, lost in despair.

35. Between BOOKS and Dreams

In the quiet hours before dawn's first light,
We huddle close, friends bound tight,
Under the weight of textbooks and endless notes,
Our whispered fears float like ghostly boats.
In the hostel, where laughter and sighs entwine,
We share stories of dreams, yours and mine.
Scraping by with coins, meals shared in jest,
Financial struggles, a never-ending test.
Being a boy, stoic mask worn well,
Hiding worries, tales untold to foretell.
Parents' calls met with reassurances bright,
Shielding them from sleepless nights.
In moments rare, between the rush and race,
Nostalgia's gentle touch, a soft embrace.
Memories of home, of simpler days,
Haunt the present in a nostalgic haze.
Yet in these bonds, in struggles shared,
Lies a strength, a love, a hope repaired.
Between the lines of pressure and strain,
Friendships flourish, easing the pain.

36. Rise again

In the shadows of yesterday's results, we stand,
Not broken, but forged by the fire's hand.
Dreams of white aprons, of saving lives,
In our hearts, the passion still thrives.
The path we tread is tough and steep,
But within us, our dreams we keep.
Failures may knock, doubts may rise,
Yet, our spirit soars towards the skies.
For every moment we felt the sting,
Is a step closer to the joy it'll bring.
To wear the white coat, to heal, to mend,
With knowledge and care, lives to defend.
Together we march, our goals aligned,
In each other's strength, hope we find.
We'll burn the midnight oil, we'll strive,
In the pursuit of dreams, we'll come alive.
Remember, it's not the fall that defines,
But the will to get up, to break confines.
With every challenge, we grow and learn,
Towards our dream college, our hearts yearn.
So let's rise, my friends, with grit anew,
In this journey, together we pursue.
For the day will come when we proudly proclaim,

"We made it, we're doctors, we've won this game.
"Through trials and tests, we will fight,
Our future is bright, the goal in sight.
Hold tight to the dream, let determination burn,
And in those white aprons, we will all return.

37. Light of an eye

Every eye, a spark divine,
Reflects the heart's enduring flame,
A silent light, no need to name,
Through tender gaze, its truth we find.
A glow that speaks of inner grace,
In depths where secret shadows play,
A beacon bright, it leads the way,
A light of love upon each face.
The heart's true light shines ever clear,
Through eyes that hold the soul's deep gleam,
A sacred glow, a golden beam,
Dispelling doubt, dispelling fear.
In eyes alight with love's pure fire,
We see the heart, the soul's delight,
A world transformed by inner light,
A glimpse of heaven to inspire.

38. Light of the Soul

In the stillness, where shadows gather,
A flicker begins, soft and hesitant,
A light not seen but felt,
The light of the soul.
It breathes in silence, through storms,
Whispers in the chaos,
Steady and unwavering,
A flame against the night.
In the laughter of a child,
In the quiet strength of ancient trees,
In those fleeting moments
When the heart leaps, unbound.
This light, it lives in our eyes,
Reflects the infinite skies,
Unfettered, breaking chains
We didn't know we carried.
It pulses in love's gentle touch,
In kindnesses, unnoticed but profound,
In the courage found in solitude,
A voice that calms the tempest.
So, in those times when the world
Seems vast and unkind,
Turn inward,

Find the glow,
The light that never dims,
The light of the soul.

39. The Temptations of Tomorrow

In the quiet of my room, books spread wide,
Dreams weave through the pages, hope by my side.
Yet, the clock ticks on, the night grows late,
And I find myself dancing with fate.
Procrastination whispers in my ear,
Promising comfort, allaying my fear.
"One more hour, one more day," it softly sighs,
As ambition within me quietly dies.
Oh, the lure of tomorrow's embrace,
Where dreams can wait, without a trace.
But as an aspirant, my heart knows the cost,
Of moments lost, and opportunities tossed.
For in the realm of my heart's design,
Every delay is a silent decline.
To the goals I cherish, to the heights I seek,
Procrastination is a foe, silent and meek.
So rise, my spirit, awaken anew,
Bid farewell to procrastination's hue.
For in the realm where dreams take flight,
Time is the wind that sets them alight.
Let each hour, each day, be a step on the way,
To the heights I aspire, come what may.

Procrastination, I cast you aside,

For my dreams and I shall no longer hide.

In the silence of my room, books spread wide,

I weave through the pages, no longer to hide.

With each passing moment, my spirit grows strong,

Procrastination fades, as I sing my own song.

Procrastination is a sneaky thief

It steals our time and sows despair

The tasks we leave just sit and stare

A constant source of quiet grief

We say we'll start, but then delay

The minutes tick, the hours pass

Our goals are left beneath the glass

Yet hope within us finds its way

To break this cycle, we must fight

And tackle tasks without retreat

Each step we take is one more feat

A shining beacon in the night

40. Scenes from a Classroom Break : The Young Scholars' Recess

In the hushed halls of knowledge, a bell rings clear,
Signaling a break, a brief escape from fear.
Tiny hands release their grip on pens,
For a fleeting moment, they're just kids again.
Books closed with a sigh, a symphony of relief,
Whispers and giggles replace the quiet of belief.
Desks left behind, like islands in a sea,
Teens set free, in this sanctuary, they flee.
Eyes once strained by pages, now brightly shine.
In this shared breath of freedom, they find their time.
Laughter bursts forth like birds taking flight,
In the tapestry of youth, woven tight.
Some gather in corners, discussing dreams and plans,
While others trace the sunlight with their hands.
A game of chase, a story shared with zest—
In these moments, their hearts find rest.
Yet shadows of exams loom not far away,
Their presence a reminder of the coming fray.
But in this break, a precious time unspools,
A glimpse of youth, before the bell of school.

As minutes tick by, the joy must end.
Books will reopen, pens will mend.
But these scenes from a classroom break remain,
A cherished respite, a sweet refrain.

.

In the hushed halls of knowledge, a bell rings clear,
Signaling a break, a brief escape from fear.
Tiny hands release their grip on pens,
For a fleeting moment, they're just kids again.
Books closed with a sigh, a symphony of relief,
Whispers and giggles replace the quiet of belief.
Desks left behind, like islands in a sea,
Teens set free, in this sanctuary, they flee.
Some chatter with friends, their laughter light,
Others glance backward, eyes gleaming bright.
A few step out, phones in hand,
Texting away in this brief, sweet span.
Some gaze across at their peers,
While others' thoughts are filled with fears.
The renowned students are sought by a few,
Clearing doubts, seeking the truth anew.
The toppers, with their knowledge vast,
Feign ignorance of what they amassed.
They lie about their study strife,
Hiding the hours spent, the midnight life.
Eyes once strained by pages, now brightly shine.
In this shared breath of freedom, they find their time.

Laughter bursts forth like birds taking flight,

In the tapestry of youth, woven tight.

Yet shadows of exams loom not far away,

Their presence a reminder of the coming fray.

But in this break, a precious time unspools,

A glimpse of youth, before the bell of school.

As minutes tick by, the joy must end.

Books will reopen, pens will mend.

But these scenes from a classroom break remain,

A cherished respite, a sweet refrain.

41. Timeless Loyalty in a Transient Age.

In a world of fleeting trends,
Where likes and follows reign,
True loyalty stands tall, my friend,
Unwavering through joy and pain.
Promises made, but often lost,
In digital whispers, faint and brief,
Yet loyalty pays the highest cost,
A quiet vow, beyond belief.
Fickle hearts, in restless flight,
Chasing dreams that quickly fade,
Loyalty remains the light,
A constant, in the games we played.
This generation seeks what's new,
In rapid tides of change and choice,
Yet loyalty, so rare and true,
Speaks softly with an ancient voice.

42. Eid ul-Adha in Palestine

In the heart of Palestine, where the olive trees sigh,
Eid ul-Adha dawns with a tear in its eye.
A day of sacrifice, of devotion, and prayer,
A day to remember, a day to care.
From Kashmir to Palestine, our hearts beat as one,
In the shadow of sorrow, beneath the same sun.
We share in your pain, in your fight for the just,
For we too, know the weight of a genocide's dust.
The streets once filled with laughter, now echo with cries,
As children search for parents beneath the clouded skies.
Tiny hands clasped in prayer, little hearts full of might,
Faces aglow with the festival's light.
Yet in their eyes, a shadow of grief,
For they celebrate in absence, beneath the olive leaf.
They find joy in each other, in the stories they tell,
In the whispers of love, in the toll of the bell.
A mother sits alone, her heart a silent scream,
Her child's laughter now a distant dream.
She lays the feast with trembling hands,
In the empty space where her child once stands.
Her prayers rise with the morning's first light, for peace,
For justice, for the end of the night.

She celebrates with hope, with tears in her eyes,
For her love transcends the boundless skies.
Remember Palestine in your duas tonight,
For their struggle is ours, in this shared plight.
From the valleys of Kashmir to the hills of Hebron,
We stand together, we carry on.
Our tears are rivers that meet in the sea,
Of unity, of strength, of a shared decree.
For we are bound by faith, by the scars we bear,
In every prayer, in every care.
In the face of despair, we find our resolve,
In the spirit of Eid, our hearts evolve.
For in every loss, there is a seed of hope,
In every struggle, a way to cope.
So let us stand, hand in hand,
For Palestine, for Kashmir, for this sacred land.
With hearts full of faith, and eyes set above,
We celebrate Eid with unyielding love.

43. Amor Doloris

In the quiet shadows of my room I stay,
A heart once whole, now in disarray.
Two loves, two stories, but one pain to bear,
The second one left scars beyond repair.
Her smile, her voice, they haunt my mind,
A love so real, yet cruelly unkind.
She took my heart and tore it apart,
Leaving me broken with a shattered heart.
I used to dream, to laugh, to play,
But now in darkness, I choose to stay.
My parents' dreams, my own lost too,
In this silent battle, I have no clue.
A fight rages on between heart and mind,
A peace, a solace, I cannot find.
I weep alone, with tears unseen,
For a love that was, and might have been.
Her photo, a relic, I hold so dear,
Wishing her voice, her words, I could hear.
But reality's chains, they bind me tight,
In this room, I dwell, out of sight.
I pen my pain, my silent cries,
In these words, my sorrow lies.
For the dreams I failed, and love I lost,

In this sea of tears, my heart is tossed.

Yet in this solitude, a hope I find,

That through these words, I might unwind.

The pain, the hurt, the silent screams,

In this poem, I'll mend my dreams.

I love you, ..., this truth I confide,

Forever and always, my heart cannot hide.

44. Echoes of absence

In the silence of the night, where echoes softly die,
I ponder on your laughter, and how it passed me by.
Six moons have come and gone, in their celestial dance,
Yet your heart remains unmoved, unyielding to romance.
You reach out in the darkness, a whisper in the wind,
Seeking what you need, then vanish once again.
My presence was a shadow, unnoticed in the light,
A fleeting thought at twilight, lost in the depths of night.
"If they don't feel your absence," a truth I can't deny,
"Then they were never happy," and I must wonder why.
Did my love not shine brightly, or was it simply faint?
A portrait left unfinished, with colors that grew quaint.
I gave my heart so freely, with every beat and sigh,
But your soul remained distant, a star in a distant sky.
I thought our love was timeless, a story to unfold,
Yet it seems it was a chapter, in a tale that's grown cold.
So now I find my solace, in knowing what is true,
That love should be a mirror, reflecting me and you.
If absence leaves no longing, then presence was a dream,
A fleeting, gentle whisper, lost in a quiet stream.
I cherish what we had, but embrace what is to come,
A future bright and open, beneath a rising sun.

For though my heart is heavy, and the nights feel long and
deep,
I know that love will find me, in the places where I weep.
So farewell to the shadows, to the echoes of the past,
I walk towards tomorrow, where love will surely last.
For if you did not miss me, then perhaps it's meant to be,
That I find a love so true, it feels my presence endlessly.

45. The love beyond reach

In silent shadows where my heart resides,
I feel a love so deep, yet distant,
She is beyond my reach,
Her absence like a tender scar.
I long for her happiness,
A selfless prayer that joy
Graces her every fleeting day.
Though she may never know,
I cherish her, despite the distance.
In my dreams, her laughter
Dances through the breeze,
A melody that soothes my soul.
Love's truest form is setting her free,
Letting her spirit find its peace.
May Allah grant her joy,
Wherever she may roam,
In letting go,
I find my heart's true home.

46. The Singular Gaze

You fall in love with a pair of eyes,
Then all other sights fade into night.
In their gaze, a world where beauty lies,
Their light alone becomes your guiding light.
Blind to all others, your heart does confide,
Bound in the spell of a singular glance.
Through their windows, your dreams softly glide,
Lost in the magic of a lover's trance.
No other eyes could ever compare,
Their sparkle, their depth, a wondrous delight.
In their reflection, love pure and rare,
A flame that burns in the darkest of night.
For in those eyes, your world does reside,
With them alone, your soul is untied.

47. The fickle Crowd

In triumph's glow, the praises gently rise,
Yet efforts meet with taunts and scornful eyes,
In sorrow, some will offer their embrace,
In joy, the world rejoices in your grace.
Through fleeting words that challenge every deed,
Let not your spirit from its course recede,
For on this path, both shadows and the light,
Reveal the hearts that stay through day and night.
When storms assail, hold steadfast to your core,
In every form, find peace forevermore,
True hearts endure through all the shifting shade,
Their loyalty through every trial displayed.
Though crowds may flock when fortune seems to smile,
It's steadfast friends who make the journey worthwhile.

48. Shadows of the Past

In shadows of the past, I dwell,
A father's voice, so strong, yet stern,
My silent cries, for love, I yearn,
A heavy heart, a tale to tell.
Your words, like echoes, still do swell,
In memories, my thoughts discern,
A distant bond, for which I burn,
Between us, barriers did swell.
Yet through the pain, a light does gleam,
A hope for peace, a silent plea,
In dreams, I find what might have been,
A chance to bridge the endless seam.
With time, perhaps, we'll find the key,
Unlock the past, set shadows free.

49. Ignoring with grace

We know the art of looking away,
To turn our eyes, our hearts astray.
But pass us by with disdain's cold kiss,
This slight, we cannot simply dismiss.
In silence, we perfect our guise,
Shielding our hearts, masking our eyes.
For though we might not meet your gaze,
In our own world, we set the blaze.
Our paths may cross in crowded rooms,
Yet in our hearts, no space for gloom.
Andaaz hume b aata hai nazar andaaz krne ka,
Lekin nagawara ho tumhe yeh humai gawara nahi.
So walk on by, if that you choose,
In your neglect, there's nothing to lose.
For we have mastered our own way,
To gracefully let go, come what may.

50. Navigating ADOLESCENCE

In shadows long, a flicker of dreams unfolds,
Adolescence blooms in the twilight's gentle hue.
Confusion thrives where once clear waters flowed,
A tapestry of pain and hope, both old and new.
Silent whispers brush against the midnight air,
A heartbeat's rhythm, lost within the storm.
In mirrors, they seek solace, faces stare,
The chaos weaves, a pattern to transform.
Yet in the labyrinth of doubt and fleeting cheer,
The soul finds strength, a beacon through the night.
Dreams dance with fears, both distant and near,
A journey from the dark into the light.
The echoes of a laugh, a tear unshed,
Juxtaposed, a symphony of highs and lows.
In fragments of the past, the future tread,
A winding path where every sorrow grows.
But see, in every fall, a rise concealed,
Enjambment of their youth's uncertain verse.
Each step, a word in the narrative revealed,
Through struggles fierce, the lines of life immerse.

51. A NEW DAWN

In the shadows of the night, I toiled and dreamed,

Beneath the flicker of hostel lights, hope softly gleamed.

Books and papers, my constant friends,

Through sleepless nights, until the struggle ends.

Sacrifices made in silent tears,

Battles fought with hidden fears.

Every sunrise, a whisper of chance,

Every sunset, a determined stance.

Now the dawn breaks, golden and bright,

The horizon of dreams within my sight.

NEET, a summit, now conquered and high,

No more tears, no more silent cry.

The hostel's whispers fade into the past,

A new journey, a future vast.

From struggle's depths, I rise anew,

A spirit unbroken, strong and true.

No longer bound by sacrifice and pain,

Freedom's breath, a sweet refrain.

A new dawn calls with promises vast,

A future bright, my dreams hold fast.

In this moment, I stand tall,

No more fear, I've conquered all.

Yet in my heart, a tender place,

I'll miss the struggle, the fervent race.

For in the trials, I found my way,

In sleepless nights and endless days.

I'll cherish the past, the journey's end,

And all the battles that made me bend.

So here I stand, my name is bright,

With dreams ahead, in morning light.

I am Moomin, and this is my song,

A new dawn has come, where I belong.

52. Echoes of Love

In the silence of the night, I weep alone,
With tears that whisper all I've never shown.
I cry for you, ..., my heart's true tone,
In memories and dreams, I'm never on my own.
Your photo's a beacon in the darkened room,
A smile that cuts through all my deepest gloom.
I hear your voice, a melody that looms,
In every whispered word, our love's perfume.
Each recording is a lifeline to the past,
A love so strong, so pure, it will always last.
In echoes of your laughter, I am cast,
Into moments where our hearts were unsurpassed.
On your birthday, though we're miles apart,
Know you reside forever in my heart.
....., my love, you are my sweetest part,
In every beat, every breath, you are my art.
Happy birthday, my love, my endless light,
In the darkness, you are my star so bright.
I love you and miss you, every night,
....., in my dreams, you hold me tight.

53. Echoes in the Café's Evening

In the café's warm and gentle glow,
We shared an evening, moments slow.
Ice cream, a kiss shared sweetly by you,
In that simple act, our love felt true.
Your hands, so delicate, fed me with care,
Biryani pizza, a bond rare.
Tender lips, a brush against my skin,
Soft cheeks that held where love begins.
Hand in mine, a touch so fine,
In your gaze, my love, I felt defined.
You smelled my perfume, whispered my name,
In those moments, our hearts aflame.
Your touch was tender, your words like song,
In your arms, I felt I belonged.
But now, where is that gentle hand?
The love that bloomed, now like shifting sand.
Eyes that once looked at me with love,
Now avoid, cold as stars above.
A silence where whispers used to be,
An echo of what we used to see.
What happened to our love so strong?
A melody turned into a silent song.

You hate to look, you refuse to speak,
Leaving me in shadows, my heart so weak.

54. Silent Tears in the WASHROOM

In the shadows of the washroom stalls,
Where echoes of silence softly fall,
Boys retreat to hide their pain,
Seeking solace from love's harsh rain.
Behind closed doors, their hearts laid bare,
They shed the tears they cannot share,
For in a world that shuns their cries,
They find a refuge, free of lies.
Branded unwanted by a callous world,
Their tender hearts in turmoil twirled,
As the most unwanted species, they stand,
Misunderstood in every land.
Their voices muted, emotions raw,
Each teardrop holds a silent law,
Of love unspoken, dreams turned gray,
In washroom corners, they find their way.
Beneath the harsh fluorescent light,
They wrestle with their inner fight,
To be the strength the world demands,
While heartbreak slips through trembling hands.
In secret spaces, boys break free,
From stoic masks the world must see,

They grieve, they mourn, they softly weep,
In washrooms, where their secrets sleep.
For love's true loss, they bear alone,
In porcelain chambers, tears are sown,
A hidden sorrow, soft and deep,
In washroom shadows, boys can weep.
Treated as if they're out of place,
Unwanted, shunned by the human race,
They don't react or voice their plea,
But weep in silence, quietly.
Their pain is cloaked, their tears unseen,
In washroom stalls, they find the mean,
To mourn the love they cannot show,
In solitude, their sorrows flow.

55. The ECHOES of Love

Can a touch of kindness spark a flame that burns?
Do whispers in the night give strength to turn?
How does a simple smile transform our darkest phase?
Is it love that lifts the heavy heart with praise?
Can shared dreams weave a tapestry so bright?
Do gentle words become the balm, our guiding light?
How does a loving gaze make courage rise in night?
Is it love that whispers, "You can take this height"?
Can tender hearts entwine to face the storm that's sown?
Do silent promises give rise to seeds we've grown?
How does a warm embrace dissolve the cold that's shown?
Is it love that breathes new life where we have flown?
Can the smallest acts of care ignite the boundless flare?
Do moments held in love expand the skies we stare?
How does love's embrace turn weakness into flair?
Is it love that transforms us, making all things fair?

56. Unseen agony

Once, they called me life, a name so sweet,

In the echo of their laughter, I found my beat.

But now I stand, a shadow in their light,

Crying silent tears in the dead of night.

I watch them smile, my heart aches with joy,

A bittersweet melody only I deploy.

Tears of happiness trickle down my face,

Yet, in her eyes, I see no trace.

Am I worth this hardship, this unending pain?

In her indifference, I find my bane.

She treats me with a cold, distant hand,

Lost in a world I can't understand.

I cry for them, but it hardly matters,

My heart, once whole, now tattered.

Her care, a distant, forgotten dream,

In this endless night, I silently scream.

But still, I hold onto the fragments of love,

Hoping for solace from the heavens above.

In their smiles, my heart will forever find,

A fleeting peace, a moment kind.

Though harsh the world, I stand tall,

For in their happiness, I give my all.

I may not be worth the pain I receive,

But in their joy, I choose to believe.

57. In the Mirror of the Soul

In the silent whispers of the night,
Where shadows dance with fleeting light,
A truth unfolds within the mind,
A riddle for the lost to find.
"I am in you and I am you,"
These words, a mystic's solemn view,
Echo through the depths of thought,
A lesson learned, but dearly bought.
To see the world through veils so thin,
To find the universe within,
One must wander far and wide,
Through valleys deep and oceans wide.
No map can guide this inward quest,
No logic soothe the restless chest,
For only when the mind is freed,
Can one embrace the sacred creed.
In madness, wisdom's seed is sown,
In chaos, secrets are bestown,
The boundaries of self erase,
Revealing love's eternal face.
So lose your mind, but find your soul,
Let cosmic rhythms take control,

For in this dance of endless grace,
We find our true and rightful place.

58. A Thousand Desires, One Love

In the garden of my heart, desires once bloomed,

Each petal a wish, a dream, a whispered thought.

A thousand passions, like stars in the night,

Shone brightly, each with its own light.

But then you appeared, a beacon so bright,

Your presence, a dawn breaking through the night.

In the warmth of your gaze, all others faded,

Like mist in the morning, gently abated.

My thousand desires, once wild and free,

Melted away, like ice in the sea.

For in knowing you, I found a truth profound,

A love so deep, where all dreams are bound.

No longer scattered, my heart now sings,

In the harmony of a single string.

Your essence, my compass, my guiding star,

In knowing you, I've discovered who we truly are.

In your presence, I've found my peace,

A love so vast, it will never cease.

For once I had a thousand desires, wild and free,

But now, in loving you, I've found the best of me.

59. Dreams to reality

If you can imagine it, you can achieve it,
Dreams can take you far,
Like a bird soaring high,
Or a journey to a star.
Tesla had a vision,
Of cars that run on light,
He believed and he created,
A future shining bright.
If you can see it in your mind,
You can make it real,
Hold on tight to your dreams,
And never lose the zeal.
With hope and determination,
And a heart that's brave and true,
The world will open up for you,
And dreams will come to view.
So, imagine and keep striving,
Believe in what can be,
For if you can imagine it,
You can achieve it, you'll see.

60. What has Happened has Happened

What has happened has happened,
The past is now gone.
Yesterday's moments,
Like a setting sun.
We can't change the past,
No matter how we try.
Time moves forward,
Like clouds in the sky.
Mistakes were made,
Lessons we've learned.
With each new day,
A fresh page turned.
So let's keep moving,
With hope in our hearts.
The future awaits,
Let's make a new start.
What has happened has happened,
It's time to move on.
Embrace the present,
For tomorrow's dawn.

61. Don't go with the Flow, be the Flow

In the rush of everyday,

We drift like leaves in streams,

Pulled along by currents strong,

Lost in distant dreams.

We follow paths well-trodden,

Afraid to make our own,

Echoes of the past surround,

A future yet unknown.

But what if we could break away,

And chart a course that's new?

Not just float along the way,

But steer with purpose true.

To rise above the river's pull,

And forge a way distinct,

To be the force that shapes the path,

Not just a chain's weak link.

In moments where the world demands,

We follow, heed, obey,

Stand firm and let your spirit guide,

Create a brand new way.

Be the wave that others chase,

The tide that sets the tone,

In the vast expanse of life,
Be the flow, your own.

62. The Light Within

In daylight, we all shine bright,
Like stained glass in the sun's light.
Colors dance and sparkles gleam,
In the warmth, we all seem serene.
But when the night starts to fall,
And darkness wraps around us all,
Our true beauty shines clear,
If we hold a light near.
For within each heart, there lies,
A glowing spark that never dies.
It lights our way, keeps us strong,
Through the night,
till the dawn.
So remember, in the dark and cold,
It's the light inside we hold,
That makes us beautiful,
warm, and kind,
A radiant glow, one of a kind.

63. The Façade

They say you're cute, a charming face,
A gentle smile, a touch of grace.
They gather 'round, pretend to care,
With words so sweet, beyond compare.
But in the shadows, whispers start,
A cruel reflection, a hidden art.
Behind your back, their true selves play,
With mocking tones, they stray away.
In public light, they hold you high,
Like stars that twinkle in the sky.
But in the dark, their colors show,
A bitter truth you come to know.
They lift you up, make you feel grand,
A precious gem in every hand.
Yet as they praise, they do the same,
To others in this shallow game.
You feel important, cherished, dear,
But doubt creeps in, your heart feels fear.
For as they smile and sing your name,
You sense the coldness of their game.
Their empty words, their hollow cheers,
Can't hide the pain, the hidden tears.
A world where masks and lies collide,

Where true intentions often hide.
So guard your heart, and know your worth,
Beyond the fleeting, shallow mirth.
For those who truly, deeply care,
Will stand by you, always there.
In this charade, don't lose your way,
Seek out the ones who truly stay.
For genuine love, sincere and rare,
Is found in hearts that truly care.

64. Eyes that speak

Today our eyes, they met again,
After so long, after the end of when.
Her gaze, it lingered, soft yet fierce,
A silent battle, emotions pierced.
My heart, once dormant, began to beat,
With every glance, it found its heat.
The world around us seemed to blur,
For in that moment, there was just her.
Her eyes, they spoke of tales untold,
Of memories warm, and nights so cold.
I felt alive, my spirit soared,
Yet pain reminded, love ignored.
She looked at me, I looked away,
Afraid of what my eyes might say.
For in her gaze, a past revived,
But truth reminded, she's not mine.
My heart awakened, full of fire,
Yet bound by fate and old desire.
To feel alive, yet still confined,
For in that look, I was resigned.
A fleeting moment, pure and raw,
Her eyes, a truth, a silent law.
That while my heart had learned to beat,

Her love was gone, a bittersweet.
So now I live with this embrace,
A heart that beats at its own pace.
For in her eyes, I found my light,
But in her absence, endless night.
Her gaze a bridge to what once was,
A time of us, a love because.
Yet as our eyes met, I discerned,
She's not mine, a lesson learned.

65. What is Pain

Pain is the echo of footsteps gone,
A hollow sound where love once shone.
It's the silent scream within your chest,
A restless soul that can't find rest.
Pain is the tear you never shed,
A pillow wet where you lay your head.
It's the smile that never reaches eyes,
A heart bound tight by unseen ties.
Pain is the memory you can't erase,
A ghost that time will not displace.
It's the yearning for a touch long missed,
A dream that fades in the morning mist.
Pain is the sight of a friend's despair,
A burden heavy you wish to share.
It's the words you choke back day by day,
A shadowed path where you lose your way.
Pain is the loss that lingers on,
A song unsung, a dawn withdrawn.
It's the cry for help that meets no ear,
A lonely fight with ceaseless fear.
Pain is the bond that time won't sever,
A wound that bleeds forever and ever.
It's the whispered prayer in the dead of night,

A fragile hope clinging tight.
Pain is the love that won't let go,
A light within that can't help but show.
It's the strength to face each breaking dawn,
A testament to a heart reborn.

66. Bravery of Dawn

In the evening's soft, calm light,
Dreams and thoughts felt just right.
Stars above in the dark sky,
Told stories as time went by.
Under the moon's gentle glow,
Hopes and fears started to show.
In my mind,
like a book,
Every answer I could look.
Paths of life spread so wide,
In this world, so big inside.
With each step,
I had to choose,
A way my heart couldn't lose.
In the quiet of the night,
Came the dawn,
clear and bright.
With bravery, I understood,
My place in time— and there I stood.

67. Always close

I want to be your clothes,
Close to you, always near,
Feeling the warmth of your body,
Sharing every breath, every tear.
If I can't be your shirt or coat,
Then let me be your socks, I pray,
Hugging your feet with every step,
With you each night and day.
I long to touch your soul,
As fabric touches skin,
To be the comfort you seek,
The safety you find within.
In the weave of life's journey,
Through every storm and lull,
Let me be the thread that's constant,
Forever close, always full.
Let me be the clothes that embrace your body,
The socks that warm your feet,
and the constant touch that comforts your soul.

68. Its going to be okay

It's going to be okay, in the stillness of the night,
When worries whisper in the dark, hold on tight,
For brighter days await their spark, shining bright,
Through storms that rage and winds that sway,
In moments when the world seems grey,
Remember this, come what may, it's going to be okay.
It's going to be okay, though shadows loom and doubts may grow,
And tears may fall like morning dew, soft and slow,
Know that strength within will flow, steady and low,
Guiding you to skies of blue, clear as day,
With every sunrise comes a chance,
To heal, to grow, to find your way, it's going to be okay.
It's going to be okay, let the stars light up your path,
And let the moon soothe your fears, calming wrath,
In the symphony of life and aftermath, follow the bath,
Find solace in the drying tears, night and day,
Believe in tomorrow, come what may,
In the gentle whispers that life conveys, it's going to be okay.

69. Laila majnu

In a land where love blooms free,
Laila and Majnu's tale, you see.
He loved her with a heart so true,
She felt it too, their love grew.
Through the desert's burning sand,
He searched for her, heart in hand.
She waited, longing in her eyes,
Their love soared beneath the skies.
But fate played its cruel part,
Tearing them, breaking their heart.
Separated, yet their love strong,
Laila and Majnu, forever belong.
In legends, their love does thrive,
A tale of passion that's alive.
Laila and Majnu, hearts entwined,
In love's embrace, forever bind.

70. What does it mean to be LOST

Lost,

A word echoing through the void,

A chasm where everything once was,

Now, nothing remains but shadows and dust

Lost everything, the tangible and the not,

Fleeting treasures, once clutched tight,

Now slipped through trembling fingers,

Disappearing into the night.

Lost mind, a labyrinth of confusion,

Thoughts swirling in a stormy sea,

Reason drowned in waves of delusion,

Clarity a distant, fading plea.

Lost in thoughts, a maze with no end,

Wandering through corridors of what-ifs,

Dreams and fears intertwined, blend,

A prisoner of the mind's own rifts.

Lost somewhere else, not here, not now,

A place unknown, a map unseen,

Feet tread paths with no guiding vow,

Wanderer in realms where none have been.

Lost in someone's memories, a haunting refrain,

Echoes of laughter, whispers of pain,

Faces and places, a bittersweet chain,
Binding the heart in a tender, sad gain.
Lost is a journey, a state, a cry,
A search for something we can't define,
In the silence, the questions lie,
What does it mean to be lost?
To be truly mine?

71. What does my Notebook see and hear when I write POEMS in it

In the quiet corner of a sunlit room,
Where whispers of dreams and shadows loom,
My notebook sits, a silent sage,
Witnessing the dance of words on each page.
It sees the flicker of my joy's bright flame,
As happiness pours in a carefree game,
Smiles and laughter, caught in ink,
Moments of bliss, too quick to blink.
It hears the echo of my sorrow's sigh,
When tears fall like rain from a cloudy sky,
Pain etched deep in every line,
A silent cry, a heart's design.
It feels the warmth of hope's embrace,
As dreams take flight in a boundless space,
Each word a step on a path unseen,
Toward a future bright, a life serene.
It listens to the murmur of sympathy's call,
In gentle verses where soft tears fall,

Compassion woven in tender strands,
A soothing touch, a helping hand.
It knows the fire of passion's blaze,
In fervent lines that set the page ablaze,
Desire and love, fierce and true,
Captured in ink, a vivid hue.
My notebook, a keeper of my soul's song,
Witnesses my journey, short and long,
From dawn of thought to dusk of dreams,
It holds my essence in flowing streams.
And if it could write, what would it say?
"Here lies a heart, unafraid to lay,
Its deepest thoughts, its brightest light,
In every poem, day and night."

72. Echoes of your Voice

In valleys deep where whispers lie,
Mountains reach and touch the sky.
An echo held within their heart,
Reminds me we're not far apart.
Your voice, it sings a sweet refrain,
A melody that soothes my pain.
In every breath, your words entwine,
In dreams, your echoes still align.
Through storms we've faced and nights so cold,
Your voice, a story yet untold.
Like rivers carving through the stone,
It's with your love I'm not alone.
Memories like stars, they brightly gleam,
In silent nights, your whispers beam.
No matter where the winds may roam,
Your echo leads my heart back home.
A mountain keeps an echo near,
Just like your voice, forever dear.
In every beat, my heart will sing,
Your love, my everlasting spring.

73. Timeless Halls of YOUTH

In the hallowed halls where laughter rings,
Where time stands still and memories sing,
We danced through days of endless light,
In classrooms bright and starry nights.
A symphony of whispered dreams,
Passed notes and shy, enchanting gleams,
In corridors where secrets lay,
Our hearts would leap, our souls would play.
The flutter of a hidden crush,
A glance, a smile, a crimson blush,
In crowded rooms, a stolen gaze,
The magic of those tender days.
Recess bells and playground games,
Where friendships bloomed and found their names,
We chased the sun, we touched the sky,
With every laugh, with every sigh.
In lunchroom chatter, bonds were sealed,
With shared delights and hearts revealed,
We wove a tapestry of care,
In every story, everywhere.
Through lessons learned and tests endured,
In every challenge, we matured,

With teachers' wisdom, guiding hands,
We mapped our futures, made our plans.
The bittersweet of summer's end,
Yet knowing we'd return again,
To halls where youth and freedom reign,
To forge new dreams, to break new chains.
As years roll by and paths diverge,
We carry forth the sacred surge,
Of friendship's light, of love's soft hue,
Of memories that bind us true.
For in those walls, our souls were tied,
In laughter, tears, and hearts confide,
A golden time, a precious key,
Unlocking all we're meant to be.
So here's to school, those golden years,
Of crushes, fun, and friendships dear,
May time be kind and ever clear,
And keep those moments ever near.

74. Whispers of fate

In the quiet dance of twilight's hue,
Where whispers of the evening breeze
Carry secrets through the trees,
I find the echo of me in you.
Stars align in a cosmic waltz,
Their silent glimmer tells our tale,
Of hearts that weathered wind and gale,
Unspoken vows, no need for false.
Beneath the moon's soft, silvery light,
Two souls converge, like rivers meet,
In timeless flow, so pure and sweet,
Destiny's path, gentle and right.
Through seasons' change, through sun and rain,
Our journey carved in nature's scroll,
With every step, we find our whole,
Bound by love, through joy and pain.
In dreams, we wander hand in hand,
Through fields of gold, under skies so blue,
A bond that time itself renews,
A love that's written in the sand.
So here we stand, in silent grace,
A story woven by the stars,
Two hearts that found where they belong,

Maybe we were meant to be,
A fate fulfilled, a perfect song.

75. Reflections in autumn

I am the season of autumn,
You hope to see me bloom.
I am a hidden star in daylight,
You call for my shine.
You ask me often,
Why don't I smile more?
But have you ever felt The dampness in my eyes?
Have you ever tried?
Many nights I've stayed awake,
What was a dream is now a lingering thought,
Full of hopes I wove a dream,
Never did it come true, not once.
Maybe the flaw lies within me,
This lack resides only in my heart.

76. Whether in love or not

In whispers of twilight, where shadows dance and play,
A question lingers softly, as night melts into day.
In the quiet moments, where moon and stars align,
The heart speaks in riddles, through poetry and time.
Is it love that lights the path, or a fleeting, tender spark?
Does the soul yearn in silence, or sing songs in the dark?
In every breath, a secret, in every glance, a clue,
The answer hides in twilight, between the old and new.
So ask again, dear seeker, let curiosity ignite,
For the heart's true tale unfolds not in day, but in night.
Is it love you see reflected, or a dream yet to be?
The mystery remains, like a whisper in the sea.

Author's Biography

Moomin Bashir, hailing from the picturesque village of Kongamdara in Baramulla, Kashmir, is a young poet with a profound love for words and an unwavering commitment to the art of healing. At 16, while preparing for a future in medicine, Moomin finds solace in the intricate dance of language, weaving emotions into verses that explore love, youth, and the raw spectrum of human experience. His writing reflects the beauty of optimism, the edge of cynicism, and the deep introspection of a keen observer. Balancing the realms of poetry and science, Moomin's words invite readers to journey through the delicate interplay of passion, dreams, and reality.